So You Wanna Get Married? Pray Before You Say "I Do"

Samantha Pegues

CONTENTS

WE ARE ONE

In Genesis 2, God pulled a rib from the inside of Adam and formed Eve. Adam then stated that Eve was bone of his bone and flesh of his flesh. God only meant for us to become one flesh after marriage. People fail to realize that we become one flesh the moment that we have sex; not after the wedding ceremony. Therefore, we are still connected to past partners. Another person doesn't just come into your marriage when your spouse cheats. If you aren't a virgin, you bring outsiders into your marriage the moment that you say, "I do." You must renounce your connection to every previous sexual partner, repent and ask God for forgiveness for having sex outside of marriage. God didn't instruct us not to fornicate to hurt us. It was to protect us from things that could destroy us in the future.

Prayer: Dear God. You are a merciful God. Thank you for covering our sins with your mercy and grace. Forgive us for joining ourselves with people who we aren't married to. Please break every ungodly soul tie so that my spouse and I may become one flesh and one spirit with you. Amen.

Scripture: "And don't you realize that if a man joins himself to a prostitute, he becomes one body with her? For the Scriptures say, "The two are united into one." -1 Corinthians 6:16, NLT

IN THAT ORDER

Most don't realize the seriousness of marriage. Biblically, your top priorities should be God, spouse (because husband and wife are one), then children. Therefore, if you were in a life or death situation, you should try to save your spouse before saving your children. Would you be able to do that? Your spouse also has priority over your mother and father which is why God instructs us to leave them and cling to your spouse. Would you be able to put your spouse before everyone you love with the exception of God? Women seem to have more of a problem with this than men. Would you be able to give your spouse priority over your children if they are not the biological parent?

Prayer: Father, you are so awesome! Thank you for giving us divine insight about marriages. Forgive us for jumping into relationships without out seeking your word for guidance. Lord, help us to put you first in everything we do. Draw my spouse's heart and spirit so tightly together so that we will always tend to each other's needs before tending to anyone else's needs. Help my children to understand that I love them dearly and they shouldn't feel as if they're second best. Amen.

Scripture: "Therefore a man shall leave his father and mother and be joined to his wife, and they shall become one flesh."- Genesis 2:24, NLT

WHY WON'T YOU SUBMIT?

Submission seems to cause a lot of controversy in marriages. Ephesians 5:22-33 advises wives to submit to their husbands because the husband is the head of the wife. I almost ripped this page out of my Bible. Just kidding. God designed the man to be the head of the household even if the wife makes more money than him. You can't fully commit to a man until you submit to him. Being submissive doesn't mean that husbands should mistreat or act controlling toward their wives. Neither does is mean that women shouldn't have an opinion, goals or dreams. Men should love their wives as Christ loves the church (Ephesians 5:25). God loved the church so much that he gave up his life for her.

Marriage was the first form of ministry as God created the

family before he created the church. The husband is the pastor of the home. What kind of pastor are you marrying? Does he have a relationship with God? Is he capable of shepherding your home? If you treat the pastor of the church better than the pastor of your home, you are out of order.

Prayer: Heavenly Father. You are the greatest man I know. Thank you for being the perfect example of a husband. Forgive us for not studying your word as we should. Lord, teach my husband how to pastor our home so that I won't mind submitting to him. Teach us how to love each other the way that you love the church. Amen.

Scripture: "28 In the same way, husbands ought to love their wives as they love their own bodies. For a man who loves his wife actually shows love for himself. 29 No one hates his own body but feeds and cares for it, just as Christ cares for the church."- Ephesians 5:28-29, NLT

CAN I TRUST YOU?

Ever heard people say that God instructs us to put no trust in man? However, throughout the Bible when God said trust no man, he was either warning us not to trust man for our salvation, deliverance; things that God can only provide. We must study the context of the content. The book of Proverbs says that the heart of the husband trusts his wife. This is the only direct reference that I've found where God promotes putting trust in another person. Ladies, can your husband trust you? With the bills? With the children? With praying and interceding for him when he's weak? To be faithful? Can he trust you with his heart?

Prayer: Dear God. You are absolutely amazing! Thank you for new revelation of your word. Forgive us for not spending enough time with you. Lord, teach me how to be a Godly wife

who my husband can trust with all of his heart. You said in your

word, "Who can find a virtuous woman? For she's more valuable

than rubies?" Show my husband my value and help him to realize

that what I bring to the table is priceless and rare to find. Amen.

Scripture: "10 Who can find a virtuous and capable wife? She

is more precious than rubies. 11 Her husband can trust her, and she

will greatly enrich his life."-Proverbs 31:10-11, NLT

YOU ARE NOT ALONE

After God formed Adam, he later said that it wasn't good for him to be alone. God immediately created a garden and animals. He first gave Adam dominion over the land. Afterwards, he created Eve and called her a helper. Ladies, does your spouse want to work? Or is he lazy and expects you to be the bread winner? Men, will your spouse be willing to help financially if you can't find work?

Many singles are unaware of their purpose. It's dangerous to marry before you discover your purpose in life. Years may pass by, but you and your spouse may have to separate because you realize that God has called you into two totally different directions.

Prayer: Heavenly Father, you are the best Mentor! Thank

you for sending the Holy Spirit to guide us. Forgive us for making decisions out of our flesh. Help me to understand my purpose so that I'll choose the right helper. Give me an assignment in your kingdom so that I can use my gifts for you and even when the economy is down, I will still be able to operate in my purpose. Amen.

Scripture:" Then the LORD God said, "It is not good for the man to be alone. I will make a helper who is just right for him."-Genesis 2:1, NLT

THE COUNTERFEIT LOOKS REAL

Ever heard of the Duck Test? It's used in abductive reasoning and it states, "If it looks like a duck, quacks like a duck and walks like a duck, then it probably is a duck." implies that a person can identify unknown subjects by observing their habitual characteristics. However, the test can't be proven true in all cases. Counterfeit money looks, feels and it can even spend like real money. However, when held to the light, it's fake qualities are revealed. What does your partner look like when held to the Light?

People can imitate positive behaviors and qualities over an extended period of time. They may regularly attend church, charm you with nice gifts, and appear to be faithful and respectful. However, you must use discernment to be able to see past their actions. Many people have signed binding contracts, such as marriage licenses, because they were mesmerized and given false information from a representative. Before you sign your life away, ask

God to show you the fine print.

Prayer: Father God, your love for me is real. Teach me how to love like you. Fine tune my spirit to my spouse's. Sharpen my discernment and quickly allow me to see past the surface of people who I meet. Amen.

Scripture: "Look beneath the surface so you can judge correctly."-John 7:34, NLT

NOTHING CAN COME BETWEEN US

What God has joined together, let no man separate is one of the most misquoted scriptures in the Bible. Just because a couple marries; that doesn't mean that God joined them together. Some people joined together out of lust, for financial gain, or they just wanted to feel a sense of belonging to another individual. So, they went to a preacher and made their union legal. Most people spend months or an entire year planning for a wedding. However, they don't spend one day fasting, praying and seeking God to find out if the marriage is in his plan. So, how can God join something together that he wasn't even a part of?

Prayer: Lord, we don't even know where to start. You are best Wedding Planner! Thank you for your mercy and your grace.

Lord, forgive us for not including you in our wedding plans. Father God, if it's in your will, join my spouse and me together so that no man or woman can separate us. We realize that it's you who does the joining; not the pastor. God, draw us so tightly together that air can't even come between us. Lord, have your way in our lives. Amen.

Scripture: "Therefore, what God has joined together, let no man separate."-Mark 10:9, NKJV

MONEY MATTERS

Finances are one of the top causes of divorce. Research shows that most couples overspend during their first few years of marriage which causes a lot of debt. Others fall into debt because of a job loss or medical expenses which also causes stress on the marriage.

While money matters, it's also important to not make money your god. Some spouses overwork themselves to afford materialistic things but they neglect their family in the process. Don't be fooled. It's possible to obtain a good paying job that stresses you out and causes you to be away from your family. As a result, you're too tired to sleep with your spouse, you neglect your children; which ultimately leads to a divorce. This is why we must seek God in everything. When God places you in a stressful situation, he gives you grace and perseverance to make it through it.

Prayer: Father God, you are the greatest Financial Advisor. Forgive us for spending without consulting you first. Lord, show us your plan for our future. Lead us into the field where you desire us to work. God, it's hard to focus on you when we're worried about how we're going to survive. Cause us to live under your economy; not so that we might become rich but so that we can serve you without distraction. Amen.

Scripture: "The blessing of the Lord makes a person rich, and he adds no sorrow with it."-Proverbs 10:22, NLT

MY CHILDREN ARE A BLESSING

Did you know that many couples divorce because of the stress of raising children? Children are one of the top causes of divorce. Often, couples can't handle their children's poor behavior which causes stress to their marriage. There's often a conflict between the two about how to raise and discipline their children. Therefore, it drives a wedge between them because more than likely, one spouse is going to take the children's side. Especially, if a step parent is involved. However, if the spouses agree, the children feel as if their parent has turned their back on them for a person who is not their biological parent. So, instead of the two spouses being one, you now have two against one. Do you and your potential spouse have an agreement about how your children will be raised and disciplined?

Prayer: Dear God, you are the perfect Parent! Thank you for leaving instructions on how to raise our children. Forgive us for trying to raise them on our own. Father God, don't allow our children to follow their mother's or their father's footsteps. Help us to teach them how to follow yours. They will not be strung out on drugs nor be incarcerated. They will be calm and obedient kids who'll grow up to be great men and women of God. Our children are an asset to our marriage; not a liability. Amen.

Scripture: "Children are a gift from the LORD; they are a reward from him."-Psalm 127:3, NLT

CAN YOU KEEP UP

The Bible tells us not to be unequally yoked together with unbelievers. When animals are yoked or tied together, they must learn to walk at the same pace and into the same direction. Otherwise, one can easily get hurt or choked to death.

Job was an amazing man of God. However, his wife didn't exactly know who he was spiritually. When Job's life began to take a downfall, his wife told him to curse God and die. It's important to marry someone who can see things from a spiritual perspective and not just a physical one. Job's wife was fine as long as he was rich and healthy but as soon as trouble came, she wished death upon him. What if your spouse was in a car accident and was paralyzed? Or their body was badly burned from a fire? Would you be able to stay with them? What if you lost your job and couldn't find work? Would your spouse criticize you and leave you for someone who has money? Or would your spouse get a job to hold things down until you recovered? Is your spouse able to keep up with you spiritually? If not, your marriage will eventually choke and die.

Prayer: Lord, we are so amazed by you! Thank you for giving us the Bible which includes everything we need to know about marriages. Forgive us for not searching your word to find the answers. God, teach my spouse and me how to seek you during the good and the bad times. Help us to pray and read your word together. Strengthen our faith so that nothing, including sickness and hard times, will be able to separate us from each other or from you. Amen.

Scripture: "...How can a believer be a partner with an unbeliever?"- 2 Corinthians 6:15, NLT

EYE CANDY

Genesis 3 explains how Eve was easily persuaded into eating from the forbidden tree. Eve ate the fruit because it was pleasant to her eyes. The tree was in the midst of the other trees that Adam had to tend to in the garden. Most theologians believe that Eve wasn't that far away from Adam when the serpent was talking to her. However, Adam was more focused on work than Eve and the enemy was able to slide right between them without Adam noticing him. You can't get so busy with your job and outside activities that you neglect your spouse. All it takes is a second for the enemy to present something that looks good to your eyes and tempt you to bite into it.

We must be careful with totally relying on science to explain human nature. Science teaches us that men are moved by sight while women make most of their decisions out of emotion. Because God took a rib from the inside of Adam and formed Eve, whatever is in men is also in women. Men, may have a stronger portion of it but it resides in women as well. Some women make more decisions based on what they see rather than what they feel.

Prayer: Father God, you are an awesome Watchman! Thank you for looking out for us. Forgive us for being lazy and letting down our guard. Teach us how to be alert and how to uncover every scheme and trick of the enemy so that we're prepared when he comes. Give my spouse an appetite for only me. Amen.

Scripture: "For we walk by faith, not by sight."-2 Corinthians 5:7, NKJV

PLEASING THE FLESH

In 1 Corinthians 7, Paul talks about how spouses should fulfill each other's sexual desires. He states that you don't have authority over your body; your spouse does. Therefore, you should do your best to satisfy your spouse's sexual desires.

Paul also talks about abstaining from sex for a period of time to seek God in prayer. People with a pure bodies are able to hear God at a different level than those who are sexually active. However, the text suggests that immediately after dedicating yourself in prayer, you should start back having sex to prevent outside temptations.

Prayer: Lord, you are the greatest God. Thank you for my spouse. Help us to always satisfy each other's sexual needs. Teach me how to make love to my spouse and how to connect with my spouse's body, soul, and spirit. Give me confidence about my body so that I'm not afraid to try new things.

Teach us how to keep our sex life interesting and pleasurable. Don't let us get tired of making love to each other. Make each time feel like the first time. Amen.

Scripture: "Do not deprive each other of sexual relations, unless you both agree to refrain from sexual intimacy for a limited time so you can give yourselves more completely to prayer. Afterward, you should come together again so that Satan won't be able to tempt you because of your lack of self-control."
-1 Corinthians 7:5, NLT

A CHILD WON'T MAKE HIM STAY

Many women believe that conceiving a child with a man will cause to man to love them more and influence marriage. God promised Abraham and Sarah a son. However, they didn't believe that they would be able to conceive because of their old age. Therefore, Abraham impregnated another woman by the name of Hagar. Hagar and her son, Ismael, were able to live with Abraham and Sarah for a set period of time. However, Abraham chose Sarah over Hagar although Hagar was the mother of his child. Just because a man impregnates you, that doesn't mean that he is going to marry you.

Prayer: God, you are so wise. Forgive me for not always

consulting you before making decisions. Teach me how to discipline my body and help me understand that bringing a child into a relationship before marriage will only complicate the our lives. Amen.

Scripture: "So Abraham got up early the next morning, prepared food and a container of water, and strapped them on Hagar's shoulders. Then he sent her away with their son, and she wandered aimlessly in the wilderness of Beersheba."-Genesis 8:14, NLT

TEST DRIVE

Many couples are willing to break God's order to test the waters to determine if their potential spouse has good sex before they say, "I do." The most common response seems to be, "You don't buy a car without test driving it." Well, the most luxurious cars such are not test-driven. Many luxury cars such as Ferraris and Bentleys cannot be test- driven. Yet, consumers still purchase them because they are confident in the manufacturer's name and reputation.

God knows us better than we know ourselves. He designed us. Not only that, he has the best track record. It's amazing how we put more trust in car manufacturers than we put in God. We don't have to sleep with our potential spouse. We should have enough confidence in God and have faith that he would not give us someone who can't satisfy our needs to the fullest capacity. Let's be honest. You have chosen a mate who had bad sex. God is not a car salesman. He would not give you a lemon for a spouse. A God-ordained marriage doesn't end in divorce because of the Manufacturer (God). Marriages fall apart because someone didn't follow the owner's manual (the Bible) or they didn't keep up the regularly scheduled maintenance (fasting, prayer, consecration).

Prayer: Dear God, you are the perfect Manufacturer. You use the best materials. Thank you for designing my spouse to have all of the qualities that I need to make our marriage last. Help us to respect and control our bodies until marriage. Teach us how to please and tolerate each other. Show me how to exceed my spouse's expectations in every area. Amen.

Scripture: "9 "You parents—if your children ask for a loaf of bread, do you give them a stone instead? 10 Or if they ask for a fish, do you give them a snake? Of course not! 11 So if you sinful people know how to give good gifts to your children, how much more will your heavenly Father give good gifts to those who ask him."-Matthew 7:9-11, NLT

CAN YOU HANDLE MY WEIGHT?

It's not a sin to be in a relationship with anyone who's single. However, it can be a weight. Apostle Paul stated that he would rather remain single so that he could serve God without distractions. Maybe he knew that the call on his life was so great that having a spouse and children would have been a distraction or weight to him. Think about it. He was hardly ever home as he had to travel hundreds of miles by foot spreading the Gospel. If he had a wife, she would have probably often complained, "You spend more time at that church than you do with your own family." If he had taken his wife and children on his journeys, he would've had to stop every five minutes to address the children for complaining about being tired and asking, "Are we there yet?" These things would've been a weight for Paul.

If you were to marry a truck driver, someone in the military or even someone in ministry who travels extensively and has to spend long periods of time away from home; would you be able to carry the weight of taking care of the household? Would you be able to handle being alone and abstain from sex for long periods of time? Are you strong enough to carry their spiritual weight?

Prayer: Lord, you are the perfect God. Your strength is made perfect in our weakness. Teach us how to cast our cares upon you for your burdens are light. Help us to be each other's strength. Lord, take the load off. Amen.

Scripture: "Therefore, since we are surrounded by such a huge crowd of witnesses to the life of faith, let us strip off every weight that slows us down, especially the sin that so easily trips us up. And let us run with endurance the race God has set before us."-Hebrews 12:1, NLT

Don't Follow Your Heart

If most people were asked what steps should be followed when choosing a spouse, the majority would probably instruct you to just follow your heart. However, your heart is the last thing that should be followed when choosing a spouse. Our hearts are full of lust, hurt, loneliness and so much more. The heart can be very deceitful. Deceit is defined by Webster as behavior that is designed to fool or trick someone. Would you trust someone who is deceitful?

Prophet Jeremiah described the heart as being desperately sick. When people are desperately sick, they will cling to the closest person to them so that they won't be alone; even if the person who they're holding on to is toxic. This is why many people stay in draining and abusive relationships. Don't follow your heart. You must follow God.

Prayer: Dear God, you complete me. Heal my heart from anger, bitterness and unforgiveness. Teach me how to love myself and how to be happy and whole while I'm single. Create in me a clean heart so that I can discern clearly and love genuinely. Amen.

Scripture: "The human heart is the most deceitful of all things, and desperately wicked. Who really knows how bad it is?"-Jeremiah 17:9, NLT

TALK TO ME

Communication is extremely important. Cancer causes a miscommunication between major organs in the body. As a result, the infected person becomes weak and broken down. If the major organs' communication is totally blocked, the person dies.

Communication is a key factor that keeps marriages alive. Lack of it is a top cause for divorce. Not only is communication between the man and woman important; communication with God is a vital part of the marriage. Does your partner know how to communicate with God? Do they have a prayer life? When both partners aren't connected to God, there is always a miscommunication and confusion. Spouses either have trouble communicating with each other or one shuts down and refuses to talk out their differences. Some people refuse to go to a counselor for treatment to better their communication skills.

If you were sick and needed treatment to live, wouldn't you be willing to pay the most capable doctor that you could afford to better your chances of survival? So, why aren't we willing to spend a little to keep our marriage alive? A lot of marriages die because people refuse to receive treatment in the form of counseling, prayer, and fasting. People will spend thousands of dollars on a wedding but won't spend a dime on counseling to stay married. So you wanna get married? Pray before you say, "I do."

Prayer: Dear God, you are the Master Communicator. Thank you for speaking to us. Please forgive us for not asking you for advice first. Teach us how to spend more time with you and how to communicate effectively with you and ourselves. Help us to not be too prideful to seek counseling from an outside source. Give us wisdom in regards to who to ask for counsel during the rough times. God, make our marriage divorce-proof. Amen.

Scripture: "The way of a fool *is* right in his own eyes,

But he who heeds counsel *is* wise."-Proverbs 12:15, NKJV